Sacrifice

Poems on the Indian Arrival
in Guyana

NEW AND SELECTED POEMS

PETER JAILALL

Sacrifice
Poems on the Indian Arrival in Guyana
by Peter Jailall

Published by: In Our Words Inc./inourwords.ca

Photographs: Courtesy Ram Jagessar/indocaribbeanheritage.com

Designed by: Shirley Aguinaldo/aguinaldo.shirl@gmail.com

Editor: Sabi Jailall

Library and Archives Canada Cataloguing in Publication

Jailall, Peter, 1944-, author
    Sacrifice : poems on the Indian arrival in Guyana / by Peter Jailall. -- Revised edition.

ISBN 978-1-926926-77-3 (paperback)

    1. East Indians--Guyana--Poetry. I. Title.

PS8569.A414S33 2016   C811'.54   C2016-907084-0

All Rights Reserved. Copyright © 2010, 2017 Peter Jailall. No part of this book may be reproduced in whole or in part, in any form, or stored on any device including digital media, except with the prior written permission of the publisher. Exceptions are granted for brief quotations utilized in critical articles or reviews with due credit given to the author.

Dedicated to our Ancestors

— — —

Introduction

These poems are about our ancestors, who were brought from India from May 1838 onwards to work on the sugar plantations of British Guiana and to replace African labour. Our ancestors came to produce wealth for the British Empire, for their own families, and for the development of their new country Guiana.

They were called "coolies" first by the British planters and later that label was used freely by others, sometimes in a very derogatory way. The word "coolie" means labourer, a producer of wealth. The word has a very significant and dignified meaning because labourers are essential to nation-building. Despite humble beginnings of toil and suffering in the sugarcane fields and later in the rice fields, they gradually moved into the villages and towns becoming professionals and business people. Some remained to live and work on the sugar plantations.

We, their descendants, do have an interesting journey and a great story to tell. As a peaceful, industrious people, we adapt comfortably to new situations, new challenges, and new environments. Armed with a quiet, determined spirit, the descendants of indentured workers have maintained the culture of work to this day.

These poems attempt to describe and capture that spirit of courage, perseverance and hard work.

Peter Jailall

Coolie huts in British Guiana

Coolies working in the sugarcane fields

British landowners with East Indian 'coolie' indentured workers

Coolies at worship. Hindu rituals

Foreword

Sacrifice a word well suited to describe a collection of poems penned over two score years and marking the career of a teacher who while residing in Canada never forgot his roots or identity.

In common parlance, *sacrifice* may mean giving up what is special to oneself for the sake of something else, loss of opportunity, or pain and suffering. But as the name for a collection, the word draws on a shared sense of its etymology to limn the character of a people contributing to nation-building on the north-east or Atlantic seacoast of South America. It is a character not devoid of but requiring agency, and exemplified by the many sons and daughters of that people, whether at home or abroad, making significant contributions to various levels of society: educational, cultural, political, economical, and ideational. The very root meaning of the word *sacrifice* is to make sacred, to put before the gods or altar, or share what is valued.

In another sense, *Sacrifice* captures more than the hardiness, determination, and daringness marking many Indo-Guyanese at home and abroad. It points also to a sense of generosity and community implicit in character and associated with morally building up as does this richly textured verse fragment from Babu: *"When me gee ayu greens / Na gee me money / Because Bhagwan bless me."* The fruits of toiling by Babu and wife are not for exchange or money but are booty from *Bhagwan* (Lord). Giver of good gifts, *Bhagwan*, is rendered from the stem *bhaga* (Sanskrit), meaning bounty, fortune, wealth, prosperity. Generosity and community along with hard work and determination are constitutive of the matrix for becoming wholly persons.

A treasure trove of cultural history too, *Sacrifice* is a reminder of language—phrases and idioms—that sustained in the midst of hardship one generation, nurtured another in the context of character formation, and kept alive through retelling or using in diaspora. Those with a linguistic bent or penchant for the vernacular will quickly make or remake acquaintance with *Bhajee* (leafy greens to cook), *Baan fu wuk* (born to work), *Soak me haan wid sal wata* (soak my hand in salt water), *Me prapa wuk haad, betta* (I worked really hard, son), *married picknie* (married off my child), *me sid donk, ready fu dead* (I sit down and am ready for the end of life), *shea cum* (she is coming), *Ahbe gu bear*, (we are going to bear), *pinching a red-hot tear-me-rass pepper* (eating a piece of red hot pepper that is apt to cause stinging in the anal sphincter) and, *Abhe dis* (all of we–this = all of us, we here).

The poems also capture less than admirable cultural circumstances against which character is formed and tested: abandonment, futility, mis-education, baiting and beckoning, bigotry and racial tensions used politically to culminate in violence. They offer a glimpse of life's experience for the new Indo-Guyanese diaspora to North America—challenges no different from or similar to those faced by their ancestors departing from Madras, or Calcutta to an indentured or plantation life in the far-flung British colony on the north-easterly coast of South America.

Poetry in the service of history, culture, and the chronicling the context of character formation, *Sacrifice* is for many, if not all, a brilliant personal exposition of what we have become as persons and as a people.

Abrahim H. (Ivan) Khan
Professor of Philosophy,
University of Toronto

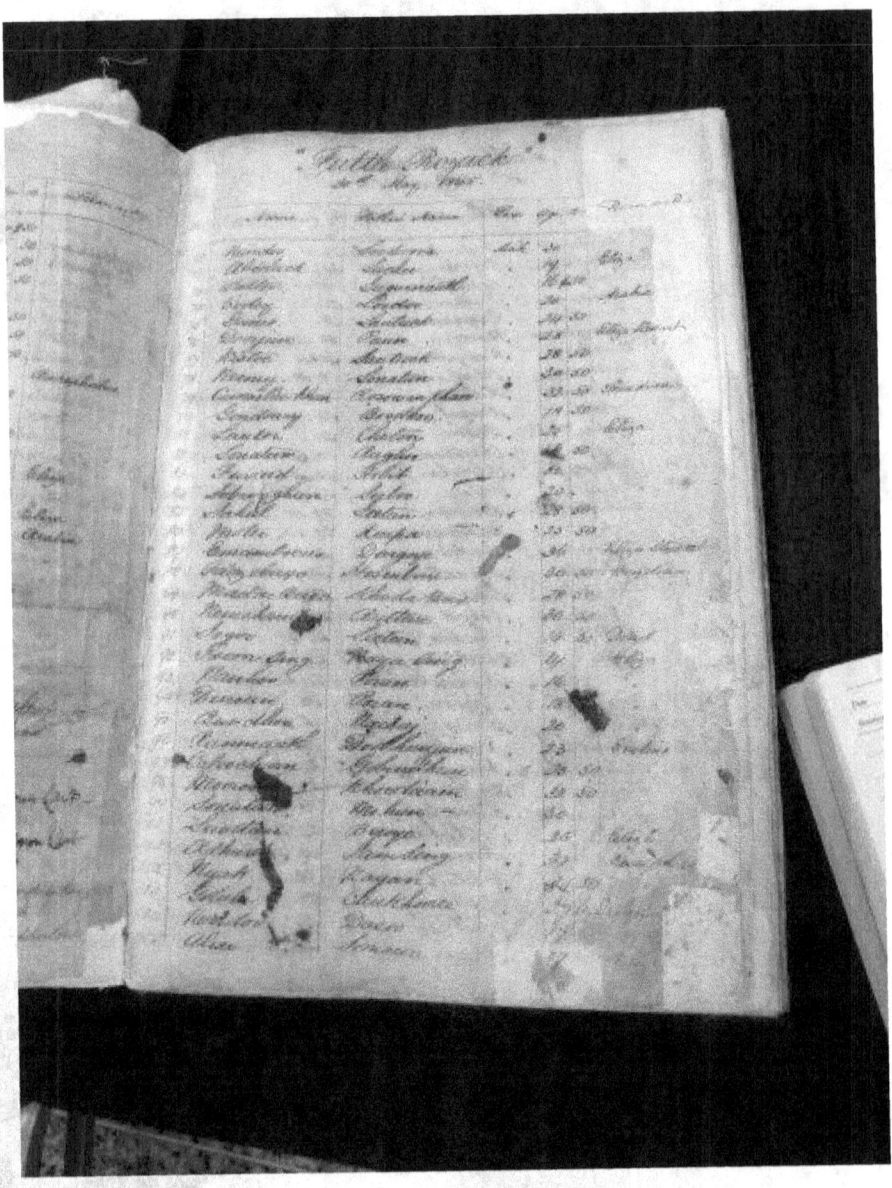

Log book of East Indian indentured workers brought in to Trinidad on the ship Futtle Rozack, 30th May 1845

A coolie family

Contents

My Forebearers

My Forebearers 13
Our Legacy 14
Catching the Last Boat 15
Baan Fu Wuk 17
Coolie Cum 19
My Ajah 21
Biaboo Babu 22
Reclaiming Gandhi Ji 23
Ahbe Dese 24
Bitta Suga 25
Without White Colgate 28
The Beauty of the Coolie 29

Sacrificial Sisters

Working with Devotion 31
Bahins Bonding 33
Khatun from Skeldon 35
My Agie's Hands 37
My Agie's Granddaughters 40
Kowsillia 41
Subhadra 42
Mis-educating Taramattie 43
Noisy Mornings 45

Parvati's Hair 46
For Better or For Worse 48
The Mule Rope 50
The Sacrifice 52
Meena's Treasures 54
The Fruit Seller 55
Dutiful Sita 56
When Nazmoon Died 57

Second Migration

Coming To Canada 59
Second Migration 60
Black Skin 61
No More Terrifying Gaze 63
Letter to Kamala-Jean 65
1962 67
When Cheddi Died 68
A Poet's Lament 70
For Julian 72
For Sash 75
The Monument 78
For OS 79
One Guyana 80
Holidaying in Guyana 82
The Rice Cutters 84
Separation 85
The Exodusters 86

My Forebearers

My Forebearers

Down the Hoogly River
In British India
Across the kala pani
To British Guiana
My brave ancestors came.

They arrived weather beaten
In brown Demerara
Cast ashore by the cunning bacra

They came in quietly
Full of innocence, full of hope
Without suitcase or passport

They came with seeds
Stitched neatly in their deep duckrie
Bigan, bindi and poi bhajee

They came barefoot, empty-handed
Ready to tramp
In the swamp.

They came with determination
And ambition
Escaping floods and droughts
Trickery and poverty
Only to face the sting
Of massa whip.

Bearing pain yet again
Still they remain.

Our Legacy

They took us away
In open ships
Dumping us off
On First Nations land

They lumped us together
Forcing us to work
And to dwell among strangers
From far away places

They instigated and disrupted
Set strife and fire
Sent in the CIA
To set the country ablaze

Then they quietly left
Setting us adrift, divided
Leaving us to heal
And rebuild.

Catching the Last Boat

On September 4th, 1955
The Last Boat left Georgetown
With 243 homesick souls
Who 'rose up' to return
To their ancestral home
Accompanied by Guyanese
Uncle Chabby Ramcharran
Interpreter, counselor and comforter.

On the last call
Just before boarding the MV Resurgent
One passenger stepped back
With a sudden change of heart –
"Na me bhaya"
He refused to go on board
He had found a new India in Guyana
With cane fields, rice fields and coconut walks
Trees laden with mangoes, tamarind
Guava and sapodilla
Mosques and temples dotting the landscape
Fast flowing rivers
Ready to swallow the ancestors' ashes.

But Gabergeela
Boarded with his adult son
Whom he snatched in the middle of the night
From his pregnant wife
With a dream of resettling
In the village of his birth.

When the boat entered the Pagla Samundar
At the horn of Africa
Gabergeela was terrified
As the boat ploughed on
Until it reached its destination.

He disembarked tired, confused, disappointed
There were no friends or relatives
To greet him
He grieved and he cried.
He had returned to a nation just born
Struggling with its own birth pains
Its leaders too busy, too reluctant
To embrace these comebackees.
Gabergeela died.

He left a sad, homesick son
To search, to wander
And to finally return to his family
In Guyana,
The land where he belonged.

Baan Fu Wuk

I man, coolie man
Baan fu wuk
Cut bush
Bun bush
Bruk dutty
Wet me haan
Wid white saliva

I man, coolie man
Baan fu wuk
Plaan rice
Cut rice
Fetch rice
Soak me toe
Wid mud wata

I man, coolie man
Baan fu wuk
Plaan cane
Cut cane
Fetch cane
Soak me haan
Wid sal wata

I man, coolie man
Baan fu wuk
Plaan bhajie
Cut bhajie
Sell bhajie

Soak me skin
Wid drain wata

I man, coolie man
Baan fu wuk
Wuk
An me wuk
Wuk
An me wuk
Til wuk friken me!

Coolie Cum

The cunning sahibs
and the haughty harkati
tricked, kidnapped and seduced me,
brought me across the Kalapani
me and me jahaji
Calling
"Cum Coolie, Cum!
Cheenie Chalay Coolie.
Cheenie Chalay!"

I arrived in British Guiana
on May 5th 1838.
Tired and sick
from the thrills
of the Pagla Samundar.

I walked bravely down the boardwalk
with me friendly Girmityas.
Work ethic intact,
expecting to make easy pisa.

I met different peoples
From continents apart
We sized each other up
Cut eye, cut eye.

Yet, we laboured together
foot to foot
Cutting cane
digging drain,
keeping out the sea.

But now, like the Harkatis,
You are kidnapping me.
Holding me hostage in Buxton.
Shooting me down in Annandale.
Demanding money and jewellery
Baiting and beckoning
"Cum coolie cum!
Coolie cum!"

My Ajah

My Ajah, handsome, strong and proud
Was an estate bound, cane-cutting coolie
banging juice for the white sahib,
from sunrise to sunset.

The hot morning sun glittered
on his aluminum saucepan,
filled with cold dhal, rice and bhajee,
which he sanayed
with his hard, cane-field fingers,
pinching a red-hot tear-me-rass pepper
as hot as the morning sun.

My Ajah staggered home at sunset
his sharp cutlish wrapped tightly
around the black corn bag
slung over his tired back.

Handsome, strong and proud,
he would return
the next day
to cut more cane for the white sahib,
and for the Empire,
on which the sun never set.

Biaboo Babu

Along Mahaica creek
Not far from Biaboo
Babu lives with his family

Gets up early
Waters the garden
While his wife cooks roti
He knows the directions of the wind
He interprets the jumbie bird's call
That heralds the coming of rain

In sun or rain
His faithful Seeta
Stands beside him
Helping him hoe
Row by row.
Freely he shares his greens
With townspeople coming to row:
"When me gee ayu greens
Na gee me money
Because Bhagwan bless me"

On late afternoons
When the creek swells
Mysterious, cold and deep
And gaulins come to roost
Babu crawls contentedly
Into his comfortable katya
With his wife Seeta.

Reclaiming Gandhi Ji

Gandhi Ji came out of India
To join us in the diaspora.
While in South Africa
He represented railroad workers.

He challenged the racists
Took their blows
Travelled first class until
They kicked him off their train.

He refused to be second class
Defied the rulers
Burned his passbook
Went to jail.

Gandhi Ji sailed back to India
Shed his Western garb
Mobilized the masses
To kick the British out.

Ahbe Dese

We are tomorrow's people
Postponed gratification is our lot
"When tomorrow comes
Not today," we say
Then we will be happy.
Tomorrow things will be brighter
By then, we will save some more
Buy the big Mahal
Pass de gyal af
Sen de baye away
Fu study dacta wuk
When e come back
We will buy de Big Motor Car
Sit in de back seat
Lal aff to enjoy
Den ahbe gu really show dem good
Meanwhile,
Ahbe gu bear, abe chayfe
Working, dreaming, waiting
Crying, fasting, praying
Do ahbe year wuk and readin'
Baaning abe belly tight
Bear worries
Tek punishment
Soak dry rotie in dhal
Til ahbe dac come back
Den everybody will say
"Shut up, leh dac talk!"
Tomorrow's people!

Bitta Suga

On the suga estate
Suga is not sweet my love
We who live there know.
We have witnessed suga's daily bitterness,
So when they ask in perfect English:
Who is marginalized?
We does sing:

"Rum kill me papa
Rum kill me ajah
Rum kill me nana
Rum kill de breadwinna
In de coolie family."

On the suga estate
Suga is not sweet my love
Ask dem cane cuttas
Dem wake up at 4'o clack
By crowing fowl kack
Fu face stink trench, black dust
Rain an buncane
Su hear dem punishment sang:

"Rum kill me papa
Rum kill me ajah
Rum kill me nana
Rum kill de breadwinna
In de coolie family."

On the suga estate
Suga is not sweet my love
Like Jesus Christ,
We carry ahbe cutlass
Around ahbe shoulda
Ben donk fu face ahbe daily crucifixion
Bearing the whip of the naked sun
On ahbe naked back
Hating ourselves, we wuk and sing:

"Rum kill me papa
Rum kill me ajah
Rum kill me nana
Rum kill de breadwinna
In de coolie family."

On the suga estate
Life is not sweet my love
Ahbe picknie baan poor, live poor and die poor
While dem dadee cut cane fu sweeten other people's lives,
Who dress well
Eat wid knife and fark
Read book, cut big English,
And ahbe picknie continued to sing:

"Rum kill me papa
Rum kill me ajah
Rum kill me nana
Rum kill de breadwinna
In de coolie family."

On the suga estate
When cane cutta retire
Dem stagga out de cane field at farty
Wid lil pension money
Not even enough fu buy lil milk and rice

All dem life
Dem wuk haad
Dem live poor
And ahbe pickney continue to sing
All de way to dem grave:

*"Rum kill me papa
Rum kill me ajah
Rum kill me nana
Rum kill de breadwinna
In de coolie family."*

So, you tell me –
who is really marginalized?

Without White Colgate

Mahadeo lived without a toothbrush
And white Colgate
Bruk and twisted datwan daily
Always chewing
The bitter end of the stick.

He squatted on his ghat
Brushing his teeth diligently
Spitting and hacking
Kach-chu, Kach-chu
Then he coolakarayed.

Hurriedly he bruk his roti
Bruk way fu de canefield
Bathing all day in black dust
But Mahadeo survived
Without toothbrush and white Colgate
Always chewing and cutting
Cutting and chewing
The bitter end of the stick.

The Beauty of the Coolie

Coolie to the estate bound
Put in a logie
Without privacy

Mek nuff picknie
Drink silane pani
Die of dysentery

Imprisoned for truancy
Beaten for lateness
Treated laka lil picknie

Fought back for liberty
Moved out of the logie
To gain respectability

Unbound coolie
Now we are free
But only if

We can see
The beauty of the coolie
In al ahbe

Sacrificial Sisters

Working with Devotion

Estate women are full of songs
Songs to dance
Songs to work
Songs to pray

They sing the choruses
over and over,
singing along
with their tape recorder.

Women washing clothes
flinging beaters
over and over
blam blam
Badam blam.

Women chunkaying curry
chun chun chun,
curry aroma floating,
drifting through
the morning dew.

Women washing hair
for early morning prayer
cold water dripping,
as they stand motionless,
meditating before their altars
under the mango trees.

Women praying faithfully,
working dutifully,
as they sing
Jai Lakshmi Ramana
Sri Lakshmi Ramana.

They sing the choruses
over and over,
singing along
with their tape recorder.

Bahins Bonding

That night Sumintra paced the floor
The moon was ripe and full
Her tired hands
Rubbing her tumbling tummy
Waiting.....crying.
Bahins from the village heard
Swarmed the house
Like an army of locusts
Rolling up sleeves
Getting ready for action
Fetched mid-wife Baby Dall
Scattered bedding
Made a comfortable bed
Washed pots
Brought firewood, limacol
Brewed bush tea
Stitched a belly ban
Sat around
Waiting... talking.

That night Sumintra paced the floor
Man Mohan escaped to the rumshop
Drinking
And waiting... for a son.

East Indian woman, Trinidad

Khatun from Skeldon

Too tired to move about at 80,
She sits down on her steps to rest.
Once, she was the fastest, cleanest weeder.
Leader of her gang.
Crop after crop,
cleaning and moulding sugarcane roots
for Booker Bros. and Company.

Now she sits
on the dung heap of estate life,
looking on, brushing flies
abandoned by Guyanese,
by friends and family.

She laments:
"Me prapa wuk haad, betta
Weed cane root
plant garden
mine fowl
mine picknie
buy house
repair house
married picknie
now, me sid donk,
ready fu dead."

My Agie's Hands

I can still see her thumbs
Dancing as they work
Her fingers rotating
In precise coordination
Those loving fingers
Bathed in coconut oil
Helping each other,
Moving like a team
Of dedicated doctors
To fix the infant's hasley.

My agie's hands
Twisting the corn bag strainer
To squeeze out the coconut milk
Leaving the kus kus dry
Then extracting the last drop
Of coconut oil
Making the chan-chee
Drier than crapaud bone.

My agie's fingernails
Harder than alligator skin
Sporting a permanent yellow
From the cutex
Of the jusya weed.

Those kurmee hands
Massaged the rice field's
Stubborn clay
Gently stroking mother earth
Opening her up for the beeya root
She, transplanting them
Giving life anew
Waiting for the autumn sun

To yield a bumper crop
My agie flexing her biceps
To make the grass knife sing
Grabbing and cutting
Handfuls of solid 79
Cleaner than the red combine.

My agie's hands
Were sowing hands
Scattering dhaan
To feed the nation
And to fatten chickens
With her che-che call.

My agie's hands
Were caressing hands
Cuddling and pressing
The pink nipples
Of the bhuri cow
Making milking music
Chun-chai, chun-chai
In her black saucepan
Sweeter than the calypso man.

My agie's hands
Had barakat
Her capstan cup, never empty
Always glittering with shillings
Those hands washed
A million cups
Clapped roti enough
To feed the world's army.

My agie's hands
Were small hands
Small hands like hers
Build big nations.

Young East Indian girls pounding grain
and fetching water

My Agie's Granddaughters

From Benares, the holy city of the Hindus
Chanting bhajans on the Hesperus
My agie's people came
Continued chanting in the cane fields
To make the work lighter
And to confuse the white sahibs.

My agie's people
With their barbed wire muscles
And ratoon stamina
Moulding cane roots
And caring cane shoots
Pinching pennies and eating slow food
Suffered and struggled for generations.

Leaving a rich legacy of hard work
And transferring their genetic blue print
To their granddaughters
Toiling today in big city towers
Far removed from the cane fields of yesterday.

Kowsillia

The bosses made demands:
"Weed cleaner!"
"Weed lower and faster!"
They had to eat standing in the rain
Or eat sitting in the scorching sun."

But Kowsillia and the women said:
"NO!"
Only to face the force of the colonial machine
That mowed her down.

March 6th, 1964 was a dreadful day
When the tractor in Leonora
Crushed Kowsillia.

All Guyana stood still
The wailing began
Followed by the long, angry procession
Moving and moulding the movement.

The people buried their heroine—
Young, beautiful, courageous.

Subhadra

Just imagine Subhadra
Early indentured sista
All the way from British India
To British Guiana.

This coolie hooman
Bold as brass
Scarce as gold
Greeted at Port Georgetown
With men singing:
"Bombai kay dulahin
aye ray
Oh Babujee!"

Just imagine Subhadra
Early pioneer sista
Moved from logie to bush house
Settling down alone
Singing back to men:
"Bird bird
Na build yu ness a corida
Yu shada gu show
In de wata."

Mis-educating Taramattie

Head Missy, Miss Barrow
Came from Barbados to teach in B.G.
She beat the children mercilessly
Her husband the sergeant major defended her cruelty.
Estate children were scared of her
She lived in the school yard
Took executive lunch hours
And left the children unattended.
Miss Barrow set work on the board
Then walked over to her house
Drank stout and ale
Dozed off in her Berbice chair
Then staggered back into the classroom.

The children whispered as she approached
"She a cum,"
Scampering to their seats.

"Get up to the board, Taramattie!" she commanded.
In fear, the little girl crept hesitatingly to the board.
She experienced difficulty
Punctuating the English sentence.

Miss Barrow bounced the child's head to the board
She fell and peed her pants
The teacher pulled off Taramattie's rumal
And dashed it on the floor.
"Wipe it up now, me maye,
Then go to the canal
And rinse your pissin' self."

Tarmattie went home crying
And never returned to school again.
She stayed home to cook and wash
While her Ma and Pa
Looked near and far
For a suitable boy.

Noisy Mornings

Brick hitting brick
Women pounding massala
Pounding pounding pounding
Grinding grinding grinding

Steel hitting steel
Men sharpening cutlish
Filing filing filing
Grinding grinding grinding

Roosters crowing
Babies bawling
Radio blaring
Whistle blowing

Calling Estate People
Calling them to rise up
Rise up!
Rise up!

Parvati's Hair

Like a busy bee
Parvati flits around the kitchen table
Balaying roti.
Her long black bouncy hair
Silhouettes through the window pane.

And no man has the right to beat her
Or pick up a sharp pair of scissors
Dash her to the ground
And cut off her locks.

Or chase her down the street
Grab her flowing tresses
Wrap it tight tight
Around his muscular hands
Swinging her light body round and round
Until she see ning ning
Paralyzing her with fear.

Or even putting her to sit
On a red ants' nest
And beat her with a black sage whip.
No!
Like Rapunzel, Paravati must be free
To let down her hair
Like honey comb.

Coolie women

For Better or For Worse

She was a daughter
Beautiful, young, obedient
And at the tender age of fifteen
Was married off
To a cattle farmer from the Creek.

A faithful child-wife
She cooked, cleaned, washed
Milked the cows
Daubed the cow pen
With a coconut broom and cow dung.

Then one day, the cattle farmer
Just to exercise his authority
With a double piece of cow rope
Beat her mercilessly
Brutalizing her tender body.

Dejected and scared
She returned to her father's house
To escape her husband's brutality.

But the words of her father
Brought her no comfort
"Baytee, people will laugh at us
That's where you belong
You have to return
They are your family now."

So accompanied by her father
She reluctantly went back
To her husband's house
Where she resumed her wifely duties
With quiet resignation.

She cooked, cleaned, washed
And daubed the cow pen
Until one day, unnoticed by her
Specks of cow dung
Spattered on one of the milk cans.

On noticing the spotted milk can
And just looking for an excuse
The angry husband
With the cow rope tripled
Descended on his young wife
With a fury unmatched.
She cowered and trembled
With each blow
Her slender body transformed
Into bloody welts
Sparing not a strip of skin.

A few days later
Her cold, curled up body
Was found behind the cowshed.
She suffered and died alone,
But this time
Papa did not know.

The Mule Rope

He always wrapped
A piece of rope
Around his body
This he needed for his job
To lead the mules back to the stables.
He was a mule driver.

But he also used the mule rope
To beat the three or more women he kept.
Woman 1: cooked his food in the logie.
Woman 2: washed his clothes.
Woman 3: pacified him in the benab
When he was angry with the others.

Then one day Woman 1 complained
To 'she sweet man, de mule driver'
About Woman 2 gossiping
And talking 'she name.'
Enraged, he ran to the broken down house
Where Woman 2 stayed
Scrambled up the steps
Bolted the kitchen door
And without a single word exchanged
He beat her mercilessly
With the mule rope
Ignoring her screams and begging
For him to stop.

Exhausted and sweating from the blows
He inflicted on the woman
He unlocked the door
Wrapped her long hair
Around his hand

Dragged her to the kitchen door.
Then kicked her down the steps.

She rolled and rolled
Unable to stop herself
With blood gushing from her mouth.
Her front teeth pitched into the air
Landing among the blood spattered
Blades of green grass.

"This will teach you a lesson
To keep your mouth shut,"
Said the mule driver under his breath
As he walked away briskly
To the logie of Woman 1,
Leaving Kamla
Unconscious on the grass.

The Sacrifice

At least once a week
Satie got a beating from her husband
For trivial reasons:
Not getting his dinner on time
Taking a long time at the market
Badmouthing his family.

She could not endure
The punishment any longer
So one day
When her husband was away
She decided to end her suffering.

She gathered the equipment –
Three heavy pieces of iron
And three pieces of rope
For the sacrifice.

With quiet determination
She led her daughters
To the Forty Feet trench
Leaving her sons behind
"They will survive."

She tied the iron
Around the waist of the five-year-old
Then coldly threw her
Into the deep, dark waters of the trench.
She watched silently
Until her daughter disappeared.

Then she tied up her four-year-old
And threw her in next
Satie watched and waited
Until she, too, struggled and sank.

Finally, she tied the iron
Around her waist
Then jumped into the same spot
Where her daughters disappeared.

For two days mother and daughters
Settled in their watery grave
At the bottom of the Forty Feet trench.
On the third day
Their bodies floated to the surface.

Satie was finally at peace
And her daughters too
Never to suffer
Like their mother did.

Meena's Treasures

Among her precious pieces of gold
At the bottom of her black suitcase
Wrapped tightly in a brown paper bag
Meena brought seeds, poi bhajee seeds
To transplant her agri-culture
On cold Canadian soil.

But on arrival, she first settled in an apartment.
So she planted a small portion of her seeds
In a box on her balcony.
The bhajee plants flourished
Green thick leaves sprung
From Meena's green thumb.
She cooked the poi bhajee with shrimps
On top of dhall and rice
Just like she did
Back in the ole country.

The Fruit Seller

Sumintra sits patiently
On her wooden peerha
Under the spreading neem tree,
Near Mahaica big bridge,
Where the river bends
And the road curves,
Selling the best tropical fruits
Grown in the land.

Smooth, round, brown sapodillas.
Short, sweet, yellow fig bananas.
White and purple star apples,
Juice running down you elbows me buddy.
Rattling green avocados.
Yellow spice mangoes.
Beautiful red cashews,
Insides white like candy floss.
Huge watermelons sounding,
Kangsing sweeter than tassa drumming.

Sumintra awaits the arrival
Of the minibus and the speedboat
On the other side of the world,
Far away from the Big Market.

Dutiful Sita

Morning breaks
Under the quiet shadows
Of tall apartment buildings
By instinct, Sita is up
Estate woman, conditioned back home
By white man's whistle
Crowing cock
Chirping bird
Demanding man
Meeting punctual Sahibs
In khaki shorts.
Now, before she heads to her factory job
She is up at five
To give her dhar
In her white enamel bathtub
Her shining thali decorated
Filled to the brim
With red plastic flowers
From Honest Ed's.
Devoted sister
Disciplined, industrious
Keeping Hindu culture alive
Nursing it on the long plane ride
To sprinkle a little bit
On Canadian soil.

When Nazmoon Died

They came for her
On that purple morning
Like hissing snakes
Set free from their black pits

They crawled on naked bellies
Among the tall black sage bush
Charged with rage and hate

Her husband sprang
Out the back window
Like a frightened cat
With one child slung on his back
Leaving Nazmoon alone
Helpless
With the unborn
Struggling
To break the wall of the womb
Paralyzed
She begged quietly: "Look at my condition
Oh! Please spare my life
For the sake of the baby inside."

But the man fired one deadly shot
Straight into her womb
Felling mother and child on the spot.

That purple morning when Nazmoon died
The baby never cried.

Second Migration

Coming To Canada

December 1969
Looking down at me
With spectacles hanging from his aquiline nose
The immigration officer said,
"So you want to go to Canada, eh?"
With a nod I replied timidly
"Yes, Sir."
"Now, what will you do if you cannot find a teaching job?"
he continued.
"I don't know, Sir," I answered nervously.
"Well," he declared gesturing like Trudeau making full use of his shoulders.
"You don't sit on your fat ass in Canada,
there are no mangoes to pick in winter, you know."
"OK, Sir," I answered politely.

March 8th 1970
Extending his hand with a smile and a friendly handshake
another immigration officer stationed at
Toronto International Airport declared,
"Congratulations and welcome to Canada,"
as he placed a stamp of approval
on my immigration papers.
"OK, Sir," I said thankfully.
I did not know then to say "Thank you"
or "You're welcome."
Well, not as yet, *eh!*

Second Migration

Aware of my traditional ways
from peasantry,
my tech-savvy son navigated the 'Net,
surfing for a suitable hotel.
"Good price!" he announced joyfully.

The next day,
we drove 500 miles
in the white winter rain
to the Holiday Inn,
in Philadelphia.

His head held high,
he stepped confidently into
the waiting elevator.

"Welcome to bourgeois living, dad!" he teased.
"It's lovely," I replied.
Then reminded him
of Dorothy's longing for Kansas.

"There's no place like home."

The ancestral home, my son.

Black Skin
(For Kamau B.)

My santan tone teecha
Read me the story –
"Scrubbing The Negro"
And whenever I see a tub of boiling water
I cringe and I cry.

Since ABC days you see,
I hated me
I always wanted to be clear –
Clear! Clear!
White! White!
Whiter than arti milk.

Not black lacka tar
Or black like bigan
Black like the ace of spades
Or black like black foul shit
Low nation chamar.

I cried, but I tried
Used white Pond's Cold Cream
Mennen's Talcum Baby Powder
Stayed in the shade
To wait and wanda
And when nobody was looking
I peeped under my arm
Just to see the progress
Of my gradual change to whiteness.

When all my efforts failed
I moved to cold white Canada
But when I returned home for a visit
They would say :
"Su yu cum back! Luk at yu
Yu mean fu tell we
Yu live su lang outside
An yu na even ketch lil culla?"

No More Terrifying Gaze

In the heat
Of the Guyanese canefields
Those blue eyes of steel
Melted me down
And drove fear
In me coolie soul.

But not now,
After I settled here
In these fields of frozen snow
I have become a fearless Canadian
With equality, dignity and courage.

Arrival of ancestors in the Caribbean celebrated in the East Indian diaspora

East Indian Coolie woman in Jamaica

Letter to Kamala-Jean

Like you,
I wanted details

The name of the ship.
The meaning of my name.
The origin of my ancestors.
Details of their punishment,
Humiliation,
Death.
Knowledge
of how they were treated,
of how they were hated.

Children jeered:
> "Coolie Gal, Your ancestors arrived
> at Port Royal
> with tails like monkeys
> which had to be cut off."

Taunted, labeled:
> "Coolie Gal
> Fit only to sell Callaloo
> On Spanish Town Road"

Kamala-Jean
You are Jamaican
East Indian
West Indian
Indo-Caribbean

Canadian.

Like you, I am not only East-Indian –
I'm Guyanese,
Caribbean and Canadian,
visible with a voice.
We have many identities.

Now I know
no more Coolie Gal, but
dignified woman –
intelligent
and strong.

1962

Run! Run! Run!
Blackman a cum

Run! Run! Run!
Coolie a cum

Run! Run! Run!
Run out de tung
Befoe de tung bun down

Run! Run! Run!
Run out de estate
Befoe e get too late

Run! Run! Run!
Blackman a fight
Coolie a fight
Al a dem a lick down
Al a dem a shoot down
Al a dem a bun down

Run! Run! Run!
Steamship a cum

Run! Run! Run!
Blackman a run
Coolie a run
Al a dem a run

Hide! Hide! Hide!
Blackman a hide
Coolie a hide
Al a dem a hide
When backra put de curfew
Pan dem backside.

When Cheddi Died

Just as he fought the oppressors
off his people's back,
so he fought off Death
but Death fought back.

And when Cheddi died,
the comrades at Freedom House cried.
They cried for their Comrade Leader –
who fought the colonialists
and taught the poor to resist.

When Cheddi died
the sugar workers cried.
They cried for their Labour Leader –
the Great Union Fighter,
who led the 80-day strike,
who challenged Big Bosses for workers' rights.

When Cheddi died,
the women cried.
They cried for their Liberator,
who helped to free Kowsilla,
crushed by a tractor,
in the heart of Leonora.

When Cheddi died,
the school children cried.
They cried for their guru,
who taught them to read,
who dispelled ignorance and greed.
Just like our modern-day Nehru.

When Cheddi died,
the people on Water Street cried.
They cried for their Nation's Father,
the Great Master Builder.
Who laboured and never surrendered,
who rebuilt a crumbling structure.

Yes, Death fought back,
putting Cheddi to rest,
but left us to continue
the fight for the oppressed.

A Poet's Lament

(First published in Guyana Chronicle February 24, 2008)

Martin is vexed, turning
Restlessly in his grave
Muttering
"Jail them quickly"
Massa day done
Colonialists lang gan
Foolishness, senseless lawlessness
Killing yuh mattee Guyanese!
Silence encouraging killing.
Shame on you!

In this firestorm
All of us tekking de heat
Drifting together
In this boat on fire
With plenty, plenty water
Flowing everywhere

Now is not the time
For vote counting, head counting
Wasting time to see
Who will blink first
Playing las lick
Like lil picknie
While picknie killing picknie
Our children trembling, screaming
Running for shelter under beds

Skulking from school.
Our feeble elders
Begging for mercy.
Progress and projects on hold.

This angry, heartless, hardcore
Marauding bunch of bandits
Creating havoc
Murdering mercilessly

Time to heed Martin's call:
"All are involved
All are consumed."
STOP THEM NOW!

For Julian

I'm brown and proud
I bruk roti
And wipe curry.

I'm brown and proud
I bruk phulowrie
And put in chatney.

I'm brown and proud
I'm not ashamed
Of my Indian ancestry.

I'm brown and proud
I'm East Indian
Not a wan-a-be.

East Indian coolies

Satyadeow (Sash) Sawh

1955 - 2006

Sash Sawh was the Guyanese Minister for Agriculture at the time he was gunned down in his home in Guyana in April 2006. He was a Canadian citizen as well and returned to his country of origin to serve in the diplomatic corps. Sawh received the highest national honour and his untimely death was mourned by Guyanese around the world.

For Sash
(June 8, 2008)

Like the Mahatma, your guru ji
You traveled, followed your people abroad
Then returned home to fight.
Indeed, you were a peaceful warrior
No coward gunman could kill
Your spirit and your ideals
You lived your life courageously
A generous spender of life's every moment
A man always on the move.

In childhood, you fled your burning house in Mahaicony, never bitter
In youth, you organized the P.Y.O. during your high school days, never afraid
In your young adult life in the A.C.G., you ploughed through deep snow in Toronto, never discouraged
Lifting your party's banner high with pride –
P.P.P. all the way
Even through the corridors of York University.

Then grounding with displaced Guyanese in Venezuela
Gathering them together for comfort
Assuring them of a better day to come
Your family, your dharampatnie always by your side
The word wife is not enough to describe Sattie's sacrifice.

And when you returned home for good
In fear, they tried to shut you down
But you weathered the Opposition Storm
Carrying your conviction
Waging war with your thunderous voice in Parliament.

Ploughing again
This time through the rice fields and flood waters of your homeland
Teaching a nation to feed itself
To stay afloat
To live in peace.
When the terrorists assassinated you, your siblings and your security guard
You called out, "Ow Gad."
Just like your Mahatma did.

And the people marched
They marched in unison, sorrow and in anger.
The cremation fire was hot,
consuming the evil around
Roaring, just like your call for liberation
The people watched
They cried and they never forgot
Your blood added fuel
to your comrades left behind.
Your memory lives on!

Long live your spirit of sustained struggle
Of courage, goodness, laughter, peace and hope!

Long live Sash Sawh –
husband, father, brother, friend and patriot!

Enmore Martyrs Monument

March for the Enmore Martyrs

The Monument

Site of our memory
And of the Enmore martyrs
Who were cut down
In the killing cane fields

Site of dripping blood from bullets
And from razor sheaves
Ratoon juks on naked feet
Site of planters' heavy boots tramping
As we ran on naked feet
Carrying heavy cane bundles
On our pagree despised heads

Site of planters perched on horseback
Throwing whip lash
On our people's back
Our timid children throwing short cane

The Monument
Site of our struggle
Our suffering
Our sacrifice

[Note: The Enmore Martyrs Monument (top, facing page) was designed by Dennis Williams and erected in June 16, 1977 on the 29th anniversary of the slaying of five workers during a strike at the Enmore Plantation on June 16, 1948.]

For OS

Like the snow that melts away
Each Spring
The leaves that blow away
Each Autumn
May your body fertilize
Mother Earth
And may your good Karma
Drift your soul away
To a peaceful resting place.

One Guyana

Guyana is my El Dorado, my desh
Not India or Africa
Not China or Portugal
England or North America
Land of cane fields, rice fields and farms
Fertilized by our ancestors' blood, sweat and tears.

Land of mighty rivers, fresh lakes
And beautiful waterfalls
Natural beauty everywhere
Land of my childhood friends
Cambridge and Campbell, Khan and Kissoon
Da Silva and Foo.

I burrowed marble holes into this land
Made the sign of the cross
On sticky wickets
Slept in rice paddy—pora straws
Under a million Guyana stars
After the lantern of the night was gone.

I paddled my own canoe
Along swift creeks and canals
Feel fu patwa in puto-puto mud wata
Mud head that I am.
I ran in open savannah
Ketch canary and bleed balata
I am glued to this land
Forever.

Map of British Guiana

Holidaying in Guyana

I sit in a breezy room
Taking in full blast the culture
That I left behind.

The swaying branches of the coconut trees
The twittering of the blue saki
The cooing of brown doves at rest
Lulling me to sleep.

I inhale the fragrance
Of white jasmine near the front gate
With the solitary Jhandi flag
Fluttering in the wind
I hear the call of a child across the fence
'Ma-ma... Ma-ma'
And I think of my own mother
Pacing the cold floor
Of her condo in Toronto.

I stare at suitcases
Under the bed
Clean and empty
Ready to go 'foreign'
Suitcases always make me sad.

Then suddenly I'm revived deep in my soul
When I hear familiar songs of my youth:
Oh Carol! I am but a fool.
The Wreck of the John B.
And yes, *Suhanay Raat*.
The church bell interrupts my nostalgia,
My meditation

A few moments of silence
Then comes on Jim Reeves:
'Some glad morning
When this life is o'er
I'll fly away.'
I ponder once more
Does it really matter
From whence I fly away?

The Rice Cutters

This gang of women
Cutting rice in the fields
Transforming labour into an art form
Cutting and chanting
Singing the Hanuman Chalisa
To make their work lighter.

Their rhythmical act
Singing, swishing
And pulling the sheaves
Make the whole performance
Into a ritual
Like doing puja.

Dressed in long sleeves
With heads wrapped
In colourful madras rumals
Protecting their bodies
From the razor sharp leaves
Of the rice stalks.

A quick lunch
From a saucepan suspended on the branch
Of a pimpla tree.
They drink black water from the canal
Sit down for a smoke
Then return to resume
The onerous task all over again.

Separation

On arrival in the far away country
I worked hard
In the open cane fields
For the white sahibs
Who were strict, loud and brutal
I endured their lashes
And curses
Punishment and poverty
Were my lot.

More than one hundred and eighty years have passed
Life is still hard
And the pay is not so great
I live in a little red house on the bank
Of a big river facing the mighty Atlantic
Yellow mangoes hang
In the golden sun
And monkeys banter in the tree tops.

I grow rice
I plant bindi and bhaji
Moulding their roots with cow dung
I rear cattle and feed my fowls
And I'm settled with my large extended family
In my new country Guyana.

I promise I will visit you someday
Search for you
And the little village
I left behind.

I think of you often
And wonder what my life would have been
If that Harkati didn't come to my door
On that rainy day.

The Exodusters

Like the Exodusters in 1897
Who moved across the mighty Mississippi,
We fled by air, by land
And by sea
Running away from the PNC.

The 1980s were bitter days
When rulers did not care
About race or creed.
If you were Afro-Guyanese
Then you should know better
They say
Especially if you belong to the WPA.

They chased you down
Beat you up
Chucked you
And even killed you
If you dared challenge them.
Smart Indo-Guyanese joined the PNC
Showed their party cards
That gave them jobs,
Promotion and protection.

Those were bitter days
When we lined up for food
Stood in the hot sun
For soap and oil
Bitter days in Hope Estate,
While on horseback
Rode in the Kabaka
More cruel and briga
Than the ole time backra.

They killed Father Darke
Shut down the press
Put critics to rest
Free speech was dead,
PNC word gospel instead.

Seniors fled to safety
Young men travelling back-track
Never went back.
A young woman crossing
The Canadian border
Suffocated in the bottom of a truck.

Exodusters still on the move
With easy U.S. visas
Fleeing from Skeldon
To Queens, to Schenectady
Deep in pain
Never to return again.

www.ingramcontent.com/pod-product-compliance
Lightning Source LLC
Chambersburg PA
CBHW070103120526
44588CB00034B/2217